BITTER-SWEET

OTHER BOOKS BY ALEXANDER ALAN STEINBACH

ৰ্বীক

When Dreamers Build
A Volume of Poems

Treatise Baba Mezia
Chapter One
(Co-author)

Sabbath Queen

What Is Judaism?

Musings and Meditations

In Search of the Permanent

BITTER-SWEET

PROSE POEMS · SONNETS · LYRICS

By ALEXANDER ALAN STEINBACH

With an Introduction by
WILLIAM W. EDEL

NEW YORK · LIBRARY PUBLISHERS · 1955

IN MEMORY OF MY BELOVED MOTHER

Sarah Goldie Steinbach

WHO TAUGHT ME HOW TO TRANSLATE
THE DREAMS OF MY HEART INTO A
STRIVING AFTER TRUTH

Acknowledgments

GRATEFUL ACKNOWLEDGMENT is made to the following publications in which some of these poems originally appeared:

American Poetry League Anthology, American Poetry Magazine, The Commonwealth, The Step Ladder, Wings, The New York Times ("Tides of Time"—January 8, 1941; "Transition"—May 5, 1941; "Song of Pain"—July 19, 1946; "Gospel"—May 2, 1954; and "Antique Shop"—November 27, 1954).

Contents

Introduction

IN THESE POEMS and paragraphs a man with calm mind and sensitive soul looks at the created world and finds it vocal of the Creator. Under the surface appearances of beauty and ugliness, design and chaos, he finds moving a deeper beauty, a subtler design. In his fingers he picks up common things, turning them about before the eye of the beholder, until common things shine with a new light, lit not only from behind, but from within. Nature is much in these sentences, winds and trees, flowers and birds, instinct with meaning which strikes down through outward seeming into spiritual reality. Because he sees beauty around through beauty within, Alan Steinbach, stretching the dimensions of his own soul, helps us to reach out for new dimensions in ours.

The form in which this book comes from the author's desk is unique. Its brief paragraphs, some only a sentence long, with no obvious connection between them, in lesser hands would have fallen apart into meaningless fragments. But Rabbi Steinbach, by a sustained spiritual exaltation of mood that lifts the reader with him, has welded the book into one, and that one a unity on a transcendent plane.

The style of the author deserves a paragraph of its own. It is at the same time disciplined and ornate. Now and again it achieves an exquisite triumph of condensation, as in: "We cannot feel the Divine touch until we have touched the Divine." Here is a philosophy in a sentence! There is rare visual imagery, too, in such phrases as "a white-hooded cloud," "snow children dance their white polka," or "a tree lying on its broad back." It is a style in which each word has its value in sound, in color, in meaning. From his youth Alan Steinbach has loved words as a painter loves the lucent hues with which he fixes memory upon canvas. He has used words with an unerring sense of nuance and beauty. At times he is a Turner, dropping sunset blaze beyond strong structural shadows—or a Birge Harrison, with all his landscape bathed in a lambent pearl-gray dawnlight—or a John Marin, evoking whole seascapes with a splash of color, a sense of gaunt form and plenty of white paper! At times he is a Whistler, scribing bold strokes against a rolling haze of lilac mist, with somewhere a butterfly atilt on a warm breeze. And sometimes in a sentence, he splashes raw Van Gogh pigments in a swirling flame of emotion. But mostly, as we read his brief, poignant paragraphs, we think of Hokusai, for there is precision and scrupulous pattern here, and behind the words is vocative life.

It seems to me that this may be a book not easily put down, one to which the reader may return again and again to re-read. Perhaps it is in such spirit as infuses this book, in such insights as these, told in such sublime words as Rabbi Steinbach uses, with such depth of understanding and compassion as is his, that the twentieth century may find its new hagiography.

WILLIAM W. EDEL
PRESIDENT, DICKINSON COLLEGE

April, 1955
Carlisle, Pennsylvania

PART ONE

Heartbeats

PROSE POEMS

&

MEDITATIONS

GOD CREATES myriads of exquisite flowers and requires of man only that he stoop and pluck them for his enjoyment. Then, after the ripened seeds fall and nestle upon the earth, God stoops down and sows them into new flowers. When the blooms appear, man does not realize they are God's tender thoughts expressing themselves. "See what lovely flowers have come from my planting," he boasts. What a pathetic display of vanity! Man is impotent to create a single drop of rain, a solitary bead of dew, a lone sunbeam, or even one feeble note in the exultant lullaby of growth that sings a hungry seed into flower.

ૐ

THE GREATNESS of a song is not that it is capable of moving a listener to tears, but that both the composer and the singer have learned how to harvest their tears and pour them into song.

ૐ

THE POET translates life into verse, the painter into pictures, the sculptor into marble, and the composer into music. All of these translations are excerpts from a cosmic text which is the primer of the Universe. Shakespeare's dramas, Milton's poetry, Michelangelo's images, Rembrandt's paintings, Beethoven's symphonies—all are interpretations of this text.

EVERY OAK TREE is a green Gothic temple with spires arching heavenward. Every acorn it produces is a tiny altar on which potential palpitant life kneels in worship.

৪৯

WE ARE ABLE to espy towering mountain summits with our eyes because peaks are within us and an inseparable part of us. We feel an affinity with ocean depths because the ocean tides and the tides of our own being originate in one and the same Source. Height and depth are the systole and diastole of our yearnings and life-throbbings. We are alpine climbers attempting to scale the rugged peaks to which our hearts' desires precariously cling. We are also mariners venturing forth in frail sloops of hope upon the storm-lashed ocean of daily existence.

৪৯

MUSIC EXTENDS the harmony of the Cosmos into the soul of man. Both partake of an indivisible unity, and their relationship is the same as the affinity between root and branch.

৪৯

A POET's thoughts are restless bees humming from flower-heart to flower-heart, gathering the sweet honey of song.

ART IS a morsel of the Infinite revealing itself to man. It awaits the advent of an individual whose sublimity of spirit and creative power of mind, coupled with the capacity to apprehend and reconstruct beauty, bring the morsel within the grasp of all men. A true work of art is a mirror of Infinity.

৶

EVERY SNOWFLAKE is a poet laureate commissioned by Nature to write a perfect white lyric on the earth's brown parchment.

৶

THE PANSIES in my garden, like little gnomes, wear impish smiles on their upturned faces. Are they harboring some secret they impart only to one another?

৶

A TIGHTLY closed bud gossips with dawns and twilights, with sun and wind and dew. Out of its whispered conversations, petals open like little wagging tongues.

৶

A FLOWER'S color is the cry it utters against the anthem of silence it heard from seed to blossoming.

WERE I a lowly blade of grass, I would reach up and yearn to become a flower. If I were a roving cloud soaring on wings of mist, I would long to fly upward and become a star. Were I a murmuring little brook, I would dream of growing into a sea; and if I became a sea, I would not rest until I wedded myself to the ocean. But being both earth-footed and soul-winged, I am content to find companionship in a humble blade of grass, beauty in a white-hooded cloud, and silver laughter in a softly purling stream. Where could one hope to find these gifts of contentment if one were a flower, or a star, or an ocean?

ɞ✦

A REDBIRD'S wings are dipped in sunrise; a robin's breast in a pool of gloaming.

ɞ✦

THE AMARANTH is a legendary flower that never fades nor dies. What an intolerable fate to be forever chained to the dizzily whirling wheel of life! What a harsh penalty to be denied the ecstasy of expanding mortality into immortality through the cycle of birth, death, and then rebirth!

ɞ✦

THERE ARE men who cringe from life as if it were a sharp javelin hurled by some malevolent hand.

THE INVINCIBLE life-impulse that courses through the earth's wrinkled veins, races also through my bloodstream. Its voyage in the soil is an ascent from root-layers of red clay to scarlet roses and red anemones. Its journey in me began with a nuptial embrace that warmed my mother's bridal bed, and it will end when a final twilight blossom will cover me with its falling saffron petals.

ॐ

LONELINESS IS a wounded dove that has strayed into a human heart and cannot find its way back to its mate.

ॐ

EVERY NEW-BORN babe is a facsimile of Eternity engraved on living clay.

ॐ

WHEN HEAVEN yearns to find a voice, the skylark's song becomes that voice. The skylark swallows a mouthful of sky and holds it captive in its little throat. It cannot return to earth until it frees the notes imprisoned in that mouthful of sky. Its tiny feathered body and the vast upspreading heights become an inclusive region sharing a common melody. The lark's aria is the will of the sky fulfilling itself.

A SUDDEN storm swooped down on black wings and blew out the gold-white tapers that flickered above the promontories of night. Hours later a lone nightingale rekindled the candles with his little flame of song, and wrapped bandages of melody around the scars inflicted by the storm.

ॐ

RAISE THE alabaster cup of life to your lips and sip the sweet wine of sweet dreams. But as you drink, remember there can be no wine without crushing the grape, and no dream without diving headlong into the pool of semi-consciousness.

ॐ

THE WORLD mirrors back to us a portrait of ourselves. What we are, we see. If we wish to discover harmony and purpose in the world, we must make life a channel through which harmony and purpose can flow freely. If we wish to see God, we must first become godly.

ॐ

MY NEIGHBOR insists he will be an agnostic until demonstrable proof is adduced for the existence of God. Whenever I see him on bended knees tending the beautiful flowers in his rock garden, I wonder how many more times he will meet God without recognizing Him.

ACCORDING TO ancient legend, Adam was an inanimate mass lying flat on the ground when God came to breathe the breath of life into him. The instant the Divine breath permeated this mass it stirred to the miracle of life, stood erect, and became an ensouled human being. From that moment, he who had belonged to earth became heir to heaven. This inheritance is the birthright of every descendant of Adam. His origin is of dust, but his soul is a temple of Divinity.

৵

MEN REAR imposing churches and temples and mosques as sanctuaries dedicated to the worship of God. Then they force Him into sectarian quarantine by proclaiming their respective altars as the only open sesame to His salvation.

৵

LOVE IS the inflow of the Divine into man. You cannot mistake the individual who becomes its talisman. A celestial coronet sits upon his brow, and an ecstatic sheen illumines his eyes.

৵

THOSE WHO espouse a theology that claims a monopoly on Divine Will for its devotees, hold a little earthen vessel into which they expect to squeeze the whole universe.

A MAN does not vindicate his religion merely by asserting, "I believe in God." Every man of whatever religion is a receptacle that holds the lineaments of Deity. Religion's noblest function is served when a man succeeds in transforming the dust-in-him into the God-in-him.

ह✿

ALL RELIGIONS have their sacred books to throw light upon the source and meaning of Divine revelation. But the book which is the spirit of man is the only instrument that records universal truth through direct contact with the Universal Soul.

ह✿

WE DO NOT lie long interred in the graves that sepulchre our bodies. We become one with the power that draws milk from earth's bosom to fructify the infant seed. We are twinned with the red flame in the ripening apple and with the sweeping blue arc that follows the eagle in flight. We become orange embers on the hearth-fires of twilight, at one with silver tassels on fields of grain, with the gleaming white foam on the Milky Way, and at one with the mysterious energy that drives the salmon a thousand miles upstream with unerring accuracy to its spawning grounds. Worms feed on the flesh, but a residue of ourselves enjoys a feast at which all created things feed.

EVERY HUMAN being is a site on which God rears His tabernacle.

୧ଈ

MUCH HAVE I seen with the seeing of my eyes and much have I heard with the hearing of my ears. But frequently I must close my eyes to behold revelations that are focused only through the telescope of the spirit. And often I hearken to truths spoken in the hushed corridors of solitude. How much there is to hear from choirs of silence! We track the Unseen and the Unseeable to its hiding place when we learn to speak and understand the language of meditation.

୧ଈ

IN THE tree of life death is only the lopping off of a branch, never the destruction of the root.

୧ଈ

FAITH IS the lamplighter who rekindles the flame in the darkened candelabrum of man's spirit.

୧ଈ

A BUD is God's smile waiting momentarily to burst into petaled laughter.

Darkness is the color of our deep loneliness. It stretches across the span that links life and death. It is the dial on the timepiece we use when we can no longer awaken to the piping of a new day.

৶

Longingly man scans the aerial ocean and yearns to attach his white dream-sails to the stellar argosy cargoed with eternity. Longingly the eternal stars gaze earthward and covet the tender passionals aglow in finite human hearts that have found love.

৶

Mountains diademed with a crown of silence are the un-fulfilled dream of seething ocean depths that yearn for the tranquillity of quiet heights. Whipped ceaselessly by the wild fury of their rampaging tides, the oceans hurl giant billows toward the heights they can never reach.

৶

Phalanx after phalanx of raindrops poured like a con-quering horde from the grey-bannered empire of the sky. A fortnight later a vast floral monarchy flew multicolored ensigns on the very terrain where the seemingly unequal battle had been joined.

WORDS LIKE "desert" and "jungle" and "wilderness" conjure up a picture of desolate wastes and brooding swamps in distant regions. But closer are the deserts and wildernesses and jungles within ourselves. Each of us is an empty vessel that needs to be filled. At times we are naked as the inscrutable desert is naked, but we know it not. Our silences are often shadows of our frustrations, but we mask our eyes in order not to see them. When shall we learn to tear away this mask of blindness that conceals our pristine Self from ourselves?

ह∾

A PRECIOUS coal is deposited on the hearth of every human being at birth. When sufficient soul-fuel is provided to enkindle the coal into a lambent flame, a key to immortality is forged in its quenchless fire.

ह∾

ONCE I watched a group of miners forsake the sun and descend into the bowels of the earth, wearing little dim lamps on their foreheads. Later they returned, weary and begrimed, drawing the hard black fruit in little cars. Then I thought of the throngs that bask in the sun's effulgence and breathe the clear air, but carry no torch into the sloping corridors where the soul's precious ore must be mined.

THE HEART is sovereign of man's physical kingdom. When it ceases to throb, Death's trumpets blare the tidings, "The king is dead." Forthwith every seed of love sowed by that heart sprouts forth like a loyal subject and exclaims, "Long live the king!"

ॐ

REACHING FOR a rose, she winced when her finger was pricked by a thorn. She scowled at the tiny globule of blood that crimsoned her skin, unmindful that the rose had bloomed only because its mother's flesh, the nourishing earth, had been lacerated by a sharp spade.

ॐ

THERE ARE inexplicable moments in life when something occurs we are certain occurred before. Words are spoken that have a familiar ring, as though we have heard them previously. Though we know the event is transpiring for the first time, or that the words are entirely new, they are mystically unstrange to us. There are eternal moments that break away from the past and invade our present. There are fragments of dreams that once reposed in a human brain, and lie dormant until the gateway of a kindred brain opens wide to let them in.

COMMUNE WITH the stars and they will sing to you like cosmic nightingales across the tremulous stillness of night.

ॐ

A PARTY of children, sauntering along a mountain path, howled with glee when they discovered several blackberry bushes. A poet who had passed that spot earlier plucked the berries with his eyes, and wrote a sonnet that will keep the fruits ripe even though the children have long since eaten them.

ॐ

As CHILDREN we are taught heaven is a celestial abode for departed souls, an elysium beyond the reach of earthly cares. Our adult rational faculties inspire the belief that heaven is not a geographical region, but an ennobling and uplifting experience. To search for heaven is far less important than *being heavenly*. It does not exist for angels but for men with all their imperfections. It is not entered after death, but during life. Man begins to build heaven the instant he pits his will against evil forces that drag men down. Every virtuous act, every effort expended for the betterment of the world, is a sun pouring light out of man's heaven. Every noble aspiration is a shooting star across the darkness of prejudice and cruelty that make heaven impossible.

CELLINI NEVER fashioned designs more beautiful than the lacy arabesques the fingers of hoarfrost etch on my window-panes.

ε∾

WHAT TRANSFIGURING music one hears in the language of a forest! Every leaf is a letter in the alphabet, every color a vowel, every bough a syllable, and every tree a word in the vocabulary spoken by the earth millennia before man appeared.

ε∾

EVERY SEED planted in the soil is a proclamation that God is making a visit to earth. Every great thought in the mind of man is a pronouncement that man is making a visit to heaven.

ε∾

IDEALS ARE convictions with sharp teeth that bite into the mind and heart, and will not let go.

ε∾

SOUL IS the Divine idiom through which God expresses the ultimate purpose He outlined for human life.

A NON-BELIEVER scoffed at the idea of Deity, and with the same breath ridiculed the suggestion that a violin can produce music without the aid of a bow and musician's fingers.

৪৯

THE REDNESS of distant stars and the redness of the loam on which my dwelling stands, are compounded of the same ingredients as the redness of my blood. Everything stems from a common matrix which is the Life of all life. The first thought-germ that made its way into a human brain, the first breath man inhaled on this earth, the first dawn that curtsied beneath the skies, the first cardinal that streaked like an arrow of red lightning over startled tree tops, the first loom that began to spin sulphur skeins for the morning sun—all are effects set in motion by a common Cause. All are links in a sequence that became manifest as the Seen only after agonizing eons of struggling as the Unseen.

৪৯

HE WHO has not passed through the crucible of suffering is a native who has never set foot off the beaten tracks of his childhood homestead. His little world has never expanded.

WHY DOES the nightingale wait for the onset of darkness before pouring out his rhapsody to the stars? Why does a tightly closed bud torment itself in a narrow dungeon before finding freedom in leaf, then in blossom, and finally in fruit? Why must the sun hemorrhage in the western sky before day can lay itself down to rest? The morning star and the morning bird know the answer. The star fuels its lamp while night still reigns, and the bird begins his serenade to dawn long before day arrives. Their light and song testify that darkness cannot vanquish those who learn how to wait.

ॐ

THROUGH HIS image implanted within me, I share with God a brief terrestrial excursion here on earth.

ॐ

MANY A HEART is callous as granite until it is broken by some overwhelming misfortune. The heart then learns how to throb pain into music, even as the bark of a tree sings under the shattering blows of an axe.

ॐ

A SUNSET gilding a grove of silver birches makes me wonder whether heaven is bringing a sacrificial offering of gold to earth, or earth a votive offering of silver to heaven.

IF THE male fern, which blossoms once a year and then only during the darkness of midnight, finds it worthwhile to produce beautiful red flowers, why should man rant at the darkness life occasionally wraps around him? Although the petals fall to earth immediately after the fern blossoms, it gives its all for the few brief moments of exultation. Here is wisdom man has not yet acquired.

੩❧

ON WHATEVER end an hourglass stands, its sand will always run out. A limited measure of time is assigned to every human being. No matter what station he attains in life, he can do nothing to prevent his quota from running out. This refers, however, only to its quantitative aspect. Qualitatively, a man's life can achieve a worthship that endures even after his hourglass has been emptied.

੩❧

WE ARE fascinated by the handiwork of man, and justifiably so. But too often we fail to revel in the loveliness that abounds beneath our feet. Magnificent indeed are the Parthenon on the Acropolis at Athens, the majestic Cathedral at Rheims, the exotic Temple of Parswanatha at Khajuraho, and scores of other structures whose grandeur leaves one breathless. But the architecture of flowers in our gardens is no less magnificent, and no less breathtaking.

BEETHOVEN ONCE wrote to a friend, "Every tree seems to say, 'Holy, Holy.'" Later he rejected a house engaged for him to write his "Ninth Symphony" because there were no trees around it. "This house will not do for me," he complained; "I love a tree more than a man." The great composer was, of course, no misanthrope. He meant his soul had to respond with music whenever he saw leaves clapping their green little hands like tinkling cymbals.

ૐ

WHENEVER I touch the supple skin of blades of grass, or stroke the satin faces of flower petals, I feel at one with the whole brotherhood of Nature. Every stalk protruding from the earth is a note in the symphony that cascades music over my whole being. A perennial song chants out of every atom of existence and unites with every atom of me.

ૐ

THE MATIN sun falls like ripened amber fruit in the grove of a waking world. Sunbeams gallop in and out of the trees, but it is for fructifying rain that the thirsty soil opens her mouth. In life's groves, smiles sit like frolicking sunrays on human lips. But tears penetrate deeply into the soul. They are sentinels standing guard over a sacred rampart where only the scarred may enter.

Two SPARKLING jewels, sunrise and moonrise, begem the brooch of heaven. One dangles from the throat of each newborn day; the other glistens on the swarthy neck of night. Both—the crimson flame and the lunar fire—cast a silver radiance on the hearth of the universe. Man, too, moves in a circle lit up by two lamps: the lamp of life and the lamp of death. He gazes with frightened eyes on the road that leads to death. But his fears will vanish if he can remember his life is a fragment of eternality that cannot be consumed by the temporary fire of death.

ॐ

OUR YEARS are slender filaments spun by the spider, Time, into a web that ultimately snares the brittle-winged moth of life.

ॐ

FOR MANY years a man neglected to replenish the fires on life's altars. Now he berates life because its lanterns are burning low.

ॐ

WE CANNOT feel the Divine touch until we have touched the Divine.

Every individual is a world too great to be toured in a single lifetime. It is impossible for a man, in his brief pilgrimage through the years, to scale the hilltops and to descend into the valleys of his total life. For a man's total life is more than the sum of his years. It is linked with a Universal Life far beyond us and yet within us. Too many stand outside this universe of total life. We need to rediscover the atlas which reveals a broader vista than the horizons we behold along the footworn highways we daily pursue.

੨੦

I am the sleeping bud and the unborn flower. I am the seed that stirred to the cry of Spring, and the helpless leaf that fell from the bough when Autumn's dream was over. I am at one with birth, and at one with things dying. I was before the beginning and shall continue to be after the end. For I am God's dream that laughs at the galloping steeds of Time.

੨੦

Look into the eyes of an individual who has lost faith in himself and you will see the portrait of a wounded stag at bay. The fear of living protrudes from his gaze like a hideous deformity.

THE BLACK tree of Sleep, growing out of the blacker roots of night, is heavy with white buds that hold the ecstasy of waking.

ॐ

How UTTERLY impoverished our world would be without music! Song is the lifeblood that stirs vitality in the heart of the universe. Should this flow cease, Cosmos would degenerate into Chaos. Night viols a lilting waltz on her ebony harp, and unnumbered meteors dance minuets to its tune. Dawn strums an anthem on carillons of light, and throngs of sunbeams pirouette merrily across the peaks of morning. Breezes run their fingers over earth's keyboard, and their melodies excite in seeds a frenzied passion to grow. I, too, am a bar of wayward music in this universal orchestration, for I have become a lute for the treble clefs that chorus out of life's harmonies and dissonances.

ॐ

MAN'S LIFE on earth is a suspension bridge between the past and the future. His present is a leash to hold in check the hounds of Time straining to race across the narrow bridge. Man draws the leash taut and wrenches the hounds back whenever they pull too vigorously. But the frothing hounds ultimately win the tug of war. Soon or late the leash snaps and they dash away never to return.

I KNOW life is brief and the years sadly fleet. But I shall not therefore cry out, "In vain, in vain. . . ." Leaves enjoy a briefer hold on life, but they do not fail to express their destiny. With what beauteous vestments they clothe themselves when summoned to their doom down the steep stairway of Autumn! Their last gasp is a raptured cry, "I have lived, I have lived; therefore I fear not death." Shall man seek less than the leaf? When he reaches the last rung on the stairway of the present, the future, a dimpled babe in the arms of Infinitude, will be the symbol of his own rebirth.

ॐ

PARADISE DOES not begin with death, but with life. The surest road to immortality is to imparadise life here on earth with deeds that will leave a legacy worthy of survival.

ॐ

MAN AND Nature woo each other, and their offspring is Art.

ॐ

WHAT IS a man? A creature preeminently greater than the portrait his acts delineate, but incomparably smaller than the limitless world of ideas and ideals stored in the treasure trove that is his mind.

He is a hero who mounts an idea and reins it firmly whithersoever it will prance, heedless of the opposition threatening to unmount him.

ॐ

Smoke ascending skyward in Ionic-like columns seems like the hands of some grotesque creature lifted up in gray prayer.

ॐ

For years she plucked pleasures like luscious fruits and stored them in life's pantry. Only when a great grief hemmed her in did she learn that suffering is a useful text in the Divine pedagogy. Her tears became a telescope that revealed what she had never understood before—the anguish and sorrow that camp on the doorstep of innumerable lives.

ॐ

Night buries its black fangs in the jugular vein of twilight and drop by drop its blood spills over the horizon into the sea. Hours later a huge white falcon claws at the throat of night and forces it to regurgitate the blood it had swallowed. A bride adorned in topaz and pearl and turquoise then tiptoes across the rose-carpeted highway and throws herself into the arms of her waiting bridegroom—Sunrise.

ETCHED UPON the banks of this river are the footprints of one who has passed this way. All of us leave traces upon the shoreline of some heart. The shadow of our presence is never lost. Sometimes it is a scar, sometimes a mark of beauty that remains. Often there is joy in the contemplation of the footprints we have left. But there are times when we trample too heavily and our footprints become grooves that disfigure the gentle slopes of the river bank.

ই

TAKE A single drop of ocean water and you will find the whole ocean condensed in that drop. Scoop a handful of desert sand and you will hold the whole desert's nakedness in the palm of your hand. All the ages that have ever been are contained in every moment that parades down the corridor of your existence. Nothing stands alone; nothing is unmated. Everything is linked to its kin or to its opposite. Every fraction, every segment, every particle, is a diminutive of a Whole from which it was separated and to which it must someday return.

ই

BEAUTY IS a brimming cup of intoxication. The more one drains the cup, the thirstier one becomes; and the greater one's thirst, the more one must drink.

IF A flower were discovered blooming from a stone, men would pause to view it out of curiosity. But magnificent flowers tinting their delicate faces at the end of a stem are passed by with scarcely a second glance.

ॐ

I WATCHED an amber-kirtled dawn glide down the hunched back of a purple mountain, and suddenly I felt as though invisible feet were standing on my own shoulders. I was not certain where the mountain ended and I began, or where I ended and the mountain began.

ॐ

LET NO man complain, "I have searched for God and not found Him." Let him rather strive to discover in what way he has hidden himself from God.

ॐ

DREAMS ARE homeless pilgrims encamped at the outer portal of consciousness. The moment the watchman relaxes his vigilance they slink into the inner courtyard. Our dreams are disguised caricatures of ourselves. They are both the candle and the light, the mask and the reality, the product of our waking and of our sleep. They steal through our slumber to tell us what we know we are, and what we prefer to be.

To HEAR and understand good music requires not only a good listening ear but also a good listening heart.

ॐ

EVERY FAILURE is a guidepost along the highway that reads: Detour—this road will not take you to your destination.

ॐ

WHEN I look into a mirror it is not only my own image that stares back at me. For I am not only my individual Self, but all mankind. I am all who have ever been, all who are now, and all who have not yet been born. Past, present and future are merely layers of Time wrapped around my Self. I carry within me the umbilical artery that unites me with the whole human family—the dead, the living, and those yet to come.

ॐ

WORDS OF comfort are a soothing lullaby that sings the sorrow of a grieving heart to sleep.

ॐ

MOUNTAIN RANGES are bouldered altars built by God for stars to kneel upon.

THE PROPHET's vison is the pulse of tomorrow throbbing in the heart of today.

੪

THE SEEING are children of light and the blind are prisoners of darkness. But even the seeing must wait for night before they can glimpse the flaming planets whirling around the sun-fire.

੪

WHEREVER THERE is a vast ocean there must be giant waves. Wherever there is great aspiring there must be raging storms.

੪

BURY A seed in the entrails of the earth. Ere long a symphony of growth will psalm out of the soil. The root pitches its tent in total darkness, but nothing can deter the stalk from boring through into the light. The seed forces the darkness to become a cup bearer for food and drink. Sit at the feet of the little seed, O my heart, and absorb its teaching! Learn that sturdy blooms are nurtured by the bitter cup life places to our lips. Joy is spurious in a heart that has not known pain. Bliss is purchased with the coin of woe; a rainbow is concealed in every tear.

HE WALKED up the cathedral steps, oblivious of the ragged beggar beseeching alms. Reverently he entered the sanctuary and knelt in prayer before the golden altar. How many idolators kneel unctuously at an altar when they can touch the hem of God's garment by lifting a helping hand to a fellow creature!

&

MANY MEN must pull themselves up by their bootstraps because somewhere along life's road they permitted earth's gravitational down-pull to gain dominion over heaven's upward beckoning.

&

SONGBIRDS ARE lyres to make vocal the poetry of the skies. Their carols clad the heights with music. Whether in the celestial bowers of blue air or in green woodlands, their songs are cosmic strands linking heaven with earth. Soar, O wings of my spirit, and learn to sing the cantata composed by heights! The silent flesh beats a pathway to earth; the aspiring spirit paves a songway to God.

&

WHEN A man wears his scars like medals, he bears testimony that his most implacable enemies have been put to rout.

A MAN's thoughts are priests marching with lighted candles in the temple of his brain. A single truth may someday become an altar at which countless millions will worship. One thought may generate sufficient power to open doors that have been tightly closed since Time began.

ॐ

THE SOUL is a projection of God into a human being. Thus, through the possession of a soul, human life extends beyond its terrestrial confines into the Allness circumferenced by Infinity.

ॐ

TREES ARE the progeny of heaven's passion to mate with the earth. Their branches are trembling arms reaching up to fondle the bosom that nursed them since birth. Their leaves are little mouths shouting green laughter at passing clouds fleeing from winds.

ॐ

GOD SIGNS His autograph with the white hieroglyphs of Winter. Even before the frosted ink dries, He begins to pen the manuscript of Spring. April blossoms complete the chapter begun by the quills of December.

A SONG unsung is a robin's blue egg that never hatches. A kind word unspoken is a pregnant seed trampled underfoot before it can give birth.

ço

FOAM-WHITE WAVES are pulsebeats of the ocean's agitated heart. Its billows are champing steeds tossing their silver manes. Swiftly they gallop outward, pulling spray-filled chariots behind them. But the moonglow of night halts their wild dash and pulls them back to the quietude of the shore. There are restless steeds racing in me. I rein them toward a more tranquil beach. But I pray they will never pull me so close to the shelter of a shore that I shall be unable to hear the chorus sung by the wave-swept sea shells.

ço

LONELY MOUNTAINS whisper to the sky, "Stoop down and sit upon my granite throne." The lonely sky answers, "Rise up from your knees and caress my heart with your summits."

ço

THE LIVES of men are hungry little mice gnawing crumbs then scampering away to hide their fright in nests of darkness.

CLOSE YOUR eyes and see! A world circumscribed only by what passes through the cornea of the eye, will not reveal the footprints of the Unseen.

ह∾

MAN HAS invented ingenious contrivances to weigh the earth, measure the ocean depths, change the profile of continents, and unravel long hidden secrets of the interplanetary world. But he has not yet learned to penetrate the abysses of his own mind. Some of the moats have been bridged, but the kingdom of mind is yet to be conquered.

ह∾

A SCHOOLHOUSE filled with children is greater than a cathedral, or mosque, or temple.

ह∾

WOULD YOU know the color of a song? Observe flowers in full bloom and you will recognize each colored petal as a musical chord in the arpeggios fluted by the earth.

ह∾

THE SONG of a throstle is a hyphen between the poetry of heaven and the poetry of earth.

NEVER WAS there a yesterday and never shall there be a tomorrow. Today is the only living flower in Time's garden. Today is the only sound that chimes on Time's eternal clock. What we call the Past is merely a name for shriveled petals fallen from a flower that once bloomed. What we call the Future is a tightly sealed bud whose imprisoned life is destined to become another Today.

ॐ

IF YOU love your enemy, you have already conquered him. If you hate your enemy, he has already conquered you. If you plan reprisals against him, you are Cain ambushing Abel.

ॐ

IF A raindrop could whisper, "There is a violet in my heart," men the world over would flock to hear and see the miracle. Peer into a violet's pistil and you will see what a reservoir of life spouted from the raindrop that watered it in early Spring.

ॐ

BIRDS IN flight are winged hours soaring over the treetops of Time. Their flutings are staccato minutes seeking a homing place in man's little nest of years.

MOUNTAINS, KNEELING like hooded monks in prayer, cry "Amen" with lips of rock and earth. What gifts they receive in answer to their prayer! Diurnally they dip their foreheads in caldrons of sunrise and in pools of sunset. Winter after winter they become mammoth maypoles around which snow-children dance their white polkas. Summer after summer they cover their flanks with green rugs for the feet of ivory-mantled clouds. Day and night they listen to secrets whispered by the pentecostal skies. How can anyone believe these kneeling monks have not a life of their own?

I ONCE read a Gaelic legend which tells that the first word God uttered to the world became a skylark. Since reading this legend, I feel God's will being translated every time a skylark's song reaches my ears.

AT TIMES there is greater truth in what we do not see than in what we see. We regard a little child and do not yet see the man, but the child *is* the man. We look upon a wan rhododendron bush and do not yet behold the flower, but the bush is the flower. Self-fulfilment is achieved more in growing than in having grown. Aspiration is a platform we build to reach something beyond ourselves.

BEAUTY IS a whip that flogs a poet until he cries his hurt into a lyric.

&

A LITTLE girl ran tearfully to her mother, heartsick at having dropped and shattered an amber kaleidoscope. How would she be able to look up into the pretty sun without it? Daily the sun opens its windows and empties rivers of gold on the earth, but how many take note? We weep over toys that fall from our hands; we discard Nature's treasures lavished upon us daily.

&

ACCORDING TO another legend, when the halcyon flew out of Noah's ark its flight was directly into the setting sun. The halcyon's plumage was dyed by the sun, and its breast was tinted with exquisite hues. In our journey out of the ark of mortality, we too soar beyond the Here into a perpetual sunrise.

&

IN NATURE'S economy there can be no wasting. If man does not use up what she creates, what she creates will use up man.

OUT OF winter's short days and long nights, out of barren earth embalmed in ice, Spring is born. Why should I fear when the cold fingers of darkness lay hold of me? I know a seed within me is waiting to burst into light.

&

SELDOM DO we arrive at an objective estimate of our fellow creature from what we see in him. Our judgments are generally dictated by what we see in our own eyes.

&

How INSUBSTANTIAL are the illusions upon which many feed! The moon reflects its lustre in a stream, and a scintillating fraction of sky seems to have descended to earth. But someone casts a pebble into the stream and instantly the moon is broken into jagged scraps.

&

IT IS not by accident that tears are shaped like precious pearls. Our laughters are fruits that have drunk their fill from goblets of sunshine. Tears are tiny wreaths placed on the grave of a buried hope. Flowers awaken at the kiss of morning light, but it is through dew-beads shaped like tears that the sparkle of the morning star is kept in their petals.

You will not respond to beauty around you until you are able to discover beauty within you.

8**

I find indisputable proof of the unity of mankind in the willingness of individuals to rise up in protest against wrongs inflicted on their fellowmen.

8**

The falling leaf spirals down and gloats to the tree, "At long last I am freed from your bondage." The tree sighs and replies, "Your bondage to me was your covenant with life; your freedom will be your death sentence."

8**

Some overwhelming cataclysm must have struck these foothills in the long ago. Their rounded breasts show naked rocks protruding like giant broken bones. The passing years have failed to weave a green cloak broad enough to cover their ugly gashes. These scars are invisible from a distance, but at close range the wounds scream into your eyes. . . . How can one approach close enough to the brain of another to learn what storms have roared behind those formidable walls of bone!

TULIPS ARE little colored lanterns hanging over patches of the earth's skin crushed by winter's boots.

કે≈

NIGHT'S MAMMOTH broom sweeps away the last amber vestiges of gloaming. But her labor is in vain. Dawn will break through night's barricades to roll out the rug into which the amber dust has been swept.

કે≈

BETTER TO shatter the precious vase than never to have known the ecstasy of worshipping at beauty's altar ere her wine ran out.

કે≈

THE VICTIM tree stands helpless as the woodman's axe cuts into her ankles. He gathers the cords and heaps them around the fireplace. But some day the woodman's axe will rust on the ground, while he sleeps in a narrow wooded tenement furnished by a brother of one of the trees he had cut down.

કે≈

MANY A heart holds a frozen lake into which tears of sorrow flowed and congealed.

THERE IS a law of divine sequence that governs all things. We see it in the ebb and flow of the tides, in the infallible movement of the planets in their courses, in the spider instinctively spinning exactly twenty-one spokes in every web she builds, in the freezing of water at thirty-two degrees Fahrenheit and in its boiling at two hundred-twelve degrees, in the burgeoning of seed into flower and flower back again into seed. . . . Human life does not escape this rigid law. Birth and death, sleeping and waking, sound and silence, laughing and weeping, light and darkness—all pay obeisance to this same law.

૭જ

TO PERCEIVE a truth requires intelligence and insight. But to *grasp* and hold on to it even at the cost of having mind and spirit seared—this is the hallmark of prophetic faith.

૭જ

MUSICIANS IN a symphony orchestra tune their instruments before the conductor's baton summons them to concerted action. Each instrument is a world of its own, but it must be in harmony with the broader world represented by the symphony. Each individual life is also a world in itself. But its highest purpose is achieved when it participates in the orchestration that produces the noblest of all symphonies—Humanity.

MANY WHO cross our path leave a trail of white spray on the dark green of life's river. Some flow out to sea alone and vanish. Others flow along with us as we wind our way toward the distant ocean.

ಶಿ

WRITE THE letters "g" and "o" and "d" on slips of paper and drop them casually on a table. After many attempts the letters may fall occasionally by mere chance in the sequence that spells G-o-d. Watch a farmer shake a pear tree in order to bring its fruits to the ground. No matter in what order they fall earthward, every pear becomes a mouthpiece proclaiming the glory of God.

ಶಿ

AT BIRTH every infant is a music box in which a particular theme-song of life is deposited. There it reposes through the years until a kindred soul, carrying a like song, calls it forth as a duet.

ಶಿ

IN EARLY childhood I believed detonating peals of thunder were deep-throated cries from denizens of the upper regions. Life has taught me silence is often more eloquent than thunderous cries.

WHENEVER YOUR eyes light on a human being, you are scanning a pathway that leads to God.

৯০

YOUR BIRTH and my birth duplicated every saffron sunrise that bled out of the womb of eternity. Your death and my death will duplicate every moonset that draws its dark drapes over the hushed catafalque of night.

৯০

TENDER BLOOMS fondling earth's wrinkled forehead are like the soft fingers of an infant caressing its mother's warm cheek.

৯০

BE NOT affrighted when night, like a black-cowled sexton, takes you by the hand and leads you through his pitch-dark catacombs. Though every passageway is paved with black tile, take heart in the certainty that a flood of dawnshine will greet you at the end of the excursion.

৯০

THAT WHICH we call Memory is a cry from life that refuses to be silenced.

FIELDS MANGLED by plows find a healing elixir in falling rain. From wounds piercing its green-haired thighs, the wet earth chants oratorios of ripening fruit and grain. This we must remember when rain falls into our lives. If floral psalms can be hummed out of earth's lacerations, man too can create carols of faith out of the aches and tribulations that torment him.

છે

MEMORY HAS the shape of a blue-black flower. Its roots are imbedded in the soil of yesterdays irrevocably lost. But the pollen seeds of those lost yesterdays are swept by winds of remembrance into the garden of the present.

છે

MEMORY IS a master painter, limning indelible pictures upon the mind's canvas. Time pilfers our years, our hopes, even our griefs. But it cannot cross the threshold that leads to the domain of Memory. Here we resuscitate the past. Here we gather once more water lilies that died, but came to life again in the pool of remembrance.

છે

THE POWERFUL hands of Memory roll away the stone forming the portal to the tomb, and bring a loved one back from the ebb tide of death's river.

THEY MET, loved, and plighted their troth; two halves attaining wholeness through matehood. After joyous years death trespassed on their union and led one away. Again they were divided into two halves. But she who survived could brave the years, knowing the two halves would some day again attain wholeness.

ॐ

TO LIVE in the past, to be hostaged to yesteryears that are lurking shadows in the nook of remembrance, is to attempt to tell time from a clock that has run down.

ॐ

THE WHOLE of life is subject to a series of invasions. Love is the invasion of the heart by a kindred heart that cannot be resisted. Compassion is an inroad on our nature by an emotion we are powerless to overcome. Convictions and ideals are incursions into our minds by invading armies of truth. Music, art and poetry scale our esthetic ramparts with regiments of melody and harmony and rhythm. Only one who yields to these invasions can hope to become a conqueror.

ॐ

PHYSICAL MAN lives and dies. Spiritual man lives and lives.

THE ARCHITECTURE that goes into the making of a human being derives its pattern from the geometry of Infinity.

WHAT LONELINESS can be compared to the aloofness of a life insensible to the tribulations of others? Such a life is a distant and solitary island so completely surrounded by a sea of self-interest that no sails from neighboring seas ever enter its waters.

ALL GARBS worn by man have changed. The nakedness of primitive man, the loin cloth of the savage, the goatskin of tribal man, the armor of the jousting knight, the velvet of the troubador, the lace of Elizabethan nobility—all have vanished. But one garb has remained changeless as the greening leaf. It is the vestment fear dons when it batters the gates of a human heart.

SINCE NIMROD'S ancient hunt began men have been fleeing from life as though savage hounds of fate were in swift pursuit. Life is not a chase nor man the quarry. If man, the hunted, would only pause long enough in his flight, he would soon discover that the hunter is—himself.

How LONG have the restless feet of vagrant winds been climbing this mountain trail with their balsam-laced sandals? I who reckon life in years, cannot venture an answer. Vainly I listen for the minstrelsy of songbirds, for their little bodies are too frail to brave these cold heights. But all is not silence here. I hearken with my soul, and through layer upon layer of stillness I can overhear neighboring mountains singing an everlasting hosanna to the listening sky.

ह

FOR MANY the dark night is not the terminus of a sun-caressed day. It is a long cry of pain waiting for the anesthesia of daybreak.

ह

BENEATH THE dark-veined eyelids of the slumbering past runs a deserted river, deep blue as an iris. Man's first desire crawled out of the river bottom and slithered across the shore of his consciousness. Again and again this primal desire struggled to retrace its steps back to the blue river, to swim uninhibited in its muddy primordial waters. But man suddenly remembered he is man and pulled the desire from its savage unrestraint back again into the dungeon of his repressed ego.

Winter cannot compete with tiny buds that keep the remembrance of Spring stored up in their hearts.

৵

I stand in awe at the alchemy that pours a spoonful of sunrise into a golden chariot and harnesses it with the glistening livery of day.

৵

November winds roam in and out of the balding trees, sobbing a melancholy elegy. They trample mounds of heart-shaped shriveled leaves orphaned from their parent boughs. The frost-bitten ground is like a clawed carcass over which packs of wolves have struggled fiercely. Only a full moon ago this was a laughing green world crooning a cadenza of burgeoning life. Now the song of decay is being piped from countless hollow reeds, while the winds dance their dance of death on naked feet.

৵

While thunder bellows like a mammoth bull in the upper corral and the storm rages with undiminishing fury, cataracts of raindrops empty their vats into the pores of the earth and whisper, "Do not fear the tempest; we shall leave a trail of tender flowers across your flooded breast."

A MAN is so many years old, but his life is Eternity old.

＄◆

DAILY GOD leads His cosmic orchestra in a superb concerto, and nightly He fills the universe with arias from whirling spheres and golden-luted stars. But man is too preoccupied with his mundane labors to give heed. What a difference when man's hurts wring a prayer from his heart! The first syllable reaches Deity. The hurts are transmuted into a rhapsody of the Divine, and the prayer becomes a song of consolation.

＄◆

SOLITUDE IS a room in the domicile that is myself. There I may enter day or night to walk with silence like a brother. There I hear the speech of deep calling unto deep. Solitude is not synonymous with being alone. The solitary eagle circling above its mountain aerie on wide convolutions of sapphire sky is less alone than a flock of hungry chattering starlings flitting from bough to bough in search of crumbs.

＄◆

THERE IS a form of bondage that sets free. Observe a tree lying on its broad back, clutching with skeleton hands for the life it lost when released from its prison of roots.

A POEM is an explosion that sends sparks of truth and melody flying like meteors in the poet's mind.

ॐ

IN THE vocabulary of the spirit words like keys and locks, months and years, clocks and calendars, do not exist. Man's spiritual life is governed by dimensions invisible to the lens of Time. They throb directly out of the eternal Heart of the Illimitable.

ॐ

WE LEARN great truths from silences. The stillness of Mount Everest is more awesome than the thunder of Niagara. The quietude of stars nestling on the breast of a lake brings us closer to the Eternal than does the roaring crescendo of a howling storm. It is in the Empire of Silence where the soul finds its homehood.

ॐ

THOUGH OUR wardrobes bulge with apparel, we remain stark and cold. Give me a single thread of song and I shall weave you a garment that will warm you night and day.

ॐ

STARS ARE opals gleaming in God's coronal.

WHO CAN decipher the secrets the wandering moon whispers nightly to the attentive earth? Perhaps this giant lantern, floating in a boundless planetary meadow, would gladly exchange its aloofness for a single hour among posies laughing to each other in an earthly garden.

ॐ

WHEN WINGED songsters usher in a new day with their triolets, every silent branch is tongued with music and every tree becomes a choral troupe.

ॐ

LITTLE BIRDS of longing fly out of the ravines in me, where they had built their nests. They flap their wings and fly aimlessly without a bough to perch upon.

ॐ

How ANGELS must envy mortal man! Being immortal and seraph-winged, it is their inexorable fate to inhabit only heaven. But man, being soul-pinioned and earth-footed, tenants both heaven and earth.

ॐ

FIRST SEED, then stalk, then flower. First thought, then idea, then action. The cycle is complete.

OUR YEARS are fragile pieces of bric-a-brac. No matter how carefully we handle them, they ultimately fall from our hands and are dashed to pieces. But all is not lost. When the fragments lie shattered at our feet, we may yet salvage a palpitant hope, a homeless song or an errant dream that has spilled out of them.

ॐ

MOST BATTLES are recorded in history according to their geographical location. The names are of little significance. On every battlefield where death stalked as high priest girdled in a red tunic woven of young men's blood, an obelisk should be erected bearing this melancholy legend, "On this mangled turf Cain the savage came to life again."

ॐ

THE SKY feels the pulse of the earth and translates it into golden music of sunlight by day and into silver recitals of starshine and moonglow by night. The earth listens to the breathing of the sky and answers with perfumed blooms that fill the white urns of day.

ॐ

WHEN A man's inner darkness is too thick to be pierced by the sun of hope, his life is in eclipse.

MANY QUILLS are used to indite Nature's anthology! But the penmanship of buds composes the most perfect of all scripts. Like patient scholars they write petaled treatises and flowered tomes to stack every shelf in earth's library.

ଛଏ

THERE ARE meanings in life deeply entrenched like roots of old trees. The fury of blustering winds shakes leaves from their parent trees, but the roots defy hurricanes.

ଛଏ

EVERY HUNGRY spirit may sit down to a sumptuous feast of stars. Only an upward flick of the eyelids and an upward tilting of the head are needed to enjoy the repast. Alas, many are too preoccupied slaving for earthly crumbs. They never gather bouquets of golden forget-me-nots that bloom in the celestial plantation.

ଛଏ

TREES CLOTHE themselves in white meditation during winter.

ଛଏ

AS TREES reach downward to draw nutriment from the soil, aged men turn backward to feed on the manna of memories.

It is hard to live in partnership with God. To attempt to live without Him is to court certain spiritual bankruptcy.

ॐ

Blind acceptance of religion is like attempting to take a picture of the spirit with a camera whose lens is hooded.

ॐ

In the Spring when wild ducks wing into the spiral plateaus of twilight, my untamed heart joins them in flight. Part of me mounts the skytrails which beckon them. Their instinct to lurch heavenward when the icefloes begin to melt, communicates itself to me. If, in reply to a command that reverberates throughout the fowl kingdom, these wild beggars learn how to converse with heights, my heart cannot be content with an earthly perch.

ॐ

The night, adorned with pendants of stars, brandishes her gems to the clouds hovering beneath her feet. But they spurn her overtures and empty their pitchers upon the humble grass below. The thirsty little green mouths drink their fill, then gratefully spread an emerald carpet for a newborn day to gambol upon.

TODAY I spied a sunrise writing poetry on a mountainside, using rhymes of laurel, hollyhocks, phlox and roses.

੩❧

RUSTLING WILLOW trees hold the echo of God's nearness in their boughs. The nocturnes lyred on their leaves are whispered invocations announcing His approach. These willows cannot flee to Thee, O Eternal, for Thou hast wedded them to earth. But hasten, hasten to them with Thy messengers of soft rain and gold-helmeted sunshine!

੩❧

WHAT LONG distances the human race has spanned in journeying from cave to skyscraper! What a short distance man has traveled from the brutish instinct of his anthropoid ancestry to the modern savagery of making H-bombs!

੩❧

NOT IN vain do life's hurts strike fire on the anvil of the heart, if a light perdures after the pain has subsided.

੩❧

A SPADEFUL of earth is a vacant house waiting to be tenanted by lilacs or forsythia or tulips.

ADAM AND Eve made girdles of fig leaves when they discovered their nakedness. How could the nude planets, capering in pirouettes around the dome of Eternity, hide their nakedness when they discovered the eye of the first telescope staring into their most intimate chambers?

❧

DREAMS are rampaging streams that break through the dykes of consciousness, then overflow the shoreline of thought into a deluge of forgetfulness.

❧

IF I can see poems sparkling in Spring blossoms, and hear Aeolian melodies fingered on the harpstrings of Summer, I need not fear the sharp cutlasses of approaching Winter. I know December is preparing floral decorations for April's vestibules at the very moment when every entrance is barred by locks of hoarfrost.

❧

FALLING SNOW is a white transfusion from the veins of heaven into the veins of earth. The white petals floating down upon trees and fields, upon turf and rooftops, are bandages to heal the earth's wounds.

TRUTH IS a pilgrim in search of the holy of holies where God, eternal and incomprehensible, waits to be known by mortal man.

৪৯

THOSE OF wavering faith might garner wisdom from the boldness of a little seed. Out of a loom entombed in the pitch-dark entrails of hard loam, it fashions an invincible dream that fulfills itself in beauty and fragrance and light. Out of its solitary cell it carves an upward path that testifies to life's continuous resurrection.

৪৯

THERE ARE men in whom there is a restless clamor of beating wings. They fly from one ephemeral goal to another, like a moth with brightly colored wings flitting from one blinding light to another.

৪৯

SPIDER-LIKE, the dreamer unwinds slender filaments of vision out of himself and hurls them again and again across chasms of skepticism and doubt. Time after time the effort fails. But once a single filament takes hold, others follow, until at last a strong web is spun as evidence that man's dream is unconquerable.

MANY SEARCH for happiness without realizing that happiness cannot be found; it must be created.

⩫

HE WHOSE dream gallery does not contain at least one masterpiece sculptured by his own life, is only a mirage in human guise.

⩫

THE OCEAN casts all dead things out of its waters, and deposits them on shore. A genuine truth-seeker disavows all that is false and fraudulent.

⩫

A WEEK before Tchaikovsky created his superb "Symphony No. 6 in B Minor" (*Pathetique*), he had written to a friend, "My faith in myself is shattered and it seems my role is ended." He did not realize that the human spirit is capable of kindling firebrands out of the ashes of frustration and defeat.

⩫

THERE CANNOT be a sea without seaweeds. There can be no rainbow without rain, no birth without pain.

STAND CLOSE to a mountain and you will see only a massive wall of earth and stone. Stand at a distance and you will see heights. Often we find fault with what we see, when the fault really lies in where we stand.

ॐ

EVERY NEW idea is waiting for a Columbus of the mind to discover it.

ॐ

THE BONES of the Past are never completely interred. They dangle from the girdle of the Present like heavy keys from the belt of a jailor guarding locked cells.

ॐ

RECENTLY I saw a painting depicting a group of men and women huddled in prayer as they watched a sloop struggling for its life in a violent storm offshore. The canvas revealed to me as much of the artist's heart as it did of his art.

ॐ

WHAT A blessed gardener you are when your understanding eyes plant a hope-seed in a heart overgrown with weeds of failure!

THE FEAR of death is frequently a secret mask for the fear of life. We are not ambushed by the speeding years. Every moment of useful living is a glorious step forward in the saga of dying.

 è❧

IF TREES barked like dogs and flowers hooted like owls, their grace and elegance would be noticed by millions who now pass by unseeing.

è❧

A BRAIN tabernacled with noble thoughts is a lighthouse piercing the darkness of many who are lost in the lowlands.

è❧

IMMORTALITY DOES not mean hoarding the present for a rainy day. The promise of life eternal means there is something deathless in man that enables him to outlive the death of his body.

è❧

WHEN I gaze on rows of tulips cupped like little pews to catch the psalms of kneeling dew, something deep within me suddenly cries out: Amen!

A DOGWOOD tree in blossom is Nature's smile translating itself into pink and white whisperings.

ॐ

WHAT IMPELS a bird to sing? Perhaps the contact of curved wings with overarching heights gives birth to silver notes that cannot be resisted. The call of heights to wings, and the answer of wings to heights, combine into an ethereal melody. Through the medium of song the bird catches and reproduces a joyous cosmic impulse which throbs out of the heartbeat of the universe.

ॐ

THE HUM of falling rain, the undertones of sea and wind, the murmur of leaves chatting with sister leaves, the chords whispered by flowers breakfasting on crystal orbs of dew, the notes chimed by twilight as it daily empties its golden basins into the ocean—all echo the World Voice whose mother tongue is music and rhythm.

ॐ

TREES ARE more than trunks and branches and leaves. They are living projections of the earth, just as children are living extensions of their parents. They are the wooded vocabulary of Nature articulating their arboreal themes to all who will draw close enough to hear.

IN EVERY human being there is a god straining to be liberated from the body's caveman heritage.

ع‌ى

HE WHO has not worn the habiliments of sorrow is blind to the incandescence of inner lamps that guide the spirit through the wilderness of pain.

ع‌ى

SOME DAY Adam, who bartered his Garden of Eden for a mouthful of fruit, will win it back with a heartful of compassion.

ع‌ى

RELIGIONS MAY differ as to what the soul is, but there can be little disagreement as to what the soul does. It kindles in every human spirit a Burning Bush whose flame can never be extinguished.

ع‌ى

EACH DAY either we die a little or are reborn a little. If Today is merely the terminus of Yesterday, we have died a little. If it is a sail daring to venture into the uncharted waters of Tomorrow, we have been reborn a little.

SINCE MAN is the product of torturous millennia of evolutionary travail, I cannot believe he is placed on this planet merely to dance like a puppet to the mad music of racing Time. He is more than a half-naked stoker shoveling the fuel of his life-blood into the roaring furnaces of the consuming years. Man is a recollection of heaven seeking homehood on earth.

&

THE WRECK of a ship involves materials that can be replaced. The wreck of a human soul is an irretrievable loss to the whole of mankind.

&

MERELY TO dream a dream is not enough. We must hoe a garden where it can be planted and nurtured, so that some day it will blossom into full bloom.

&

A WHITE paralysis has stricken the silver maple on my lawn, and all its leaves have been lanced by the spears of December. But despite its barrenness, I cannot forget this is the same tree I surprised last Spring fondling a sunrise in its arms.

When we examine the ways of Time we become aware of a striking paradox. The more it gives of itself the greater grows its domain. Seconds grow into minutes, minutes into hours, hours into days, days into weeks. . . . It binds ten years together and converts them into a decade, ten decades into a century, centuries into ages and ages into eons. The more it spends of its own substance the vaster becomes its immensity. When it touches human life, however, the formula is reversed. The more a man is touched by Time the smaller becomes his domain. The passing of every second, every minute, diminishes his remainder. And yet, the smaller his remainder becomes in Time the richer he grows for having been diminished by the passing years. Maturity is bought at a high price.

&

Neither steel girders nor the spades of Time can forge a crypt deep enough to bury the roses and the thistles that bloomed in the garden of yesteryear.

&

It is reported that when the statue of Moses was completed Michelangelo struck it sharply with a hammer and urged it to speak. Within every man, waiting for some sculptor to release it, is a sublime image greater than man himself.

THE HUMAN eye is blinded by the limitations of its own retina. Space and time are mountains it cannot hurdle. But the spirit is an astronomer. It designs a telescope with a miraculous lens that magnifies heights which are farther removed from mundane flesh than the Milky Way is distant from the lowly earth. Man gazes through this telescope, and not only does he catch a clear view of these heights; he *becomes* these heights.

ह৯

WHEN SORROW is permitted to become an obsession, it marks the triumph of weakness. He who does not turn from bereavement to the duties and challenges and responsibilities of life, surrenders to the line of least resistance. He who stops playing when a string has snapped in life's harp, reduces the flow of song into the world. He who pitches his tent in the shadow of a tombstone, defiles the sanctity of life.

ह৯

HE WHO demands proof for the existence of the soul unwittingly confesses he has missed the noblest spiritual adventure upon which life can embark. He thereby announces he is so deeply earth-manacled, he is unable to gain sufficient stature to glimpse the celestial horizons of the inner spirit.

IF ADAMANT marble can be forced to liberate glorious images through powers wielded by the sculptor, if truth can be kindled into a blazing torch by the fire of the poet, if the savage beast can be stripped of its jungle ferocity by an animal trainer, if miracles of richer growth can be coaxed from the earth through the intercession of men of science, what grandeur must be waiting to be freed in man!

રે

WHENEVER A word of hate leaves your lips, you are unsheathing a sword that will cut a wound in some human heart.

રે

EVERY MAN is a sculptor, using materials of heart and mind and spirit to hew the hard granite of human nature into higher patterns. His task is not completed until he cuts away the caveman and releases the angel.

રે

SUFFERING IS a surgeon that shuns anesthetics as its sharp scalpels cut into the sensitive cords of our hearts. But its surgery, though seamed with scars, leaves strength where there was weakness. After tears comes tranquillity. After suffering comes mellowness and humility of spirit.

RULERS MIGHT hesitate to embark upon a conquest for world dominion if they could only realize that man himself is the richest empire existing on the whole earth.

ह०

PAIN IS not the stratagem of some evil destiny bent on overthrowing us. It is the raw material out of which we carve patterns of richer personality. It is the dark mine out of which we excavate the precious ore of understanding, compassion, sympathy and forbearance. Were it not for the shadows cast in their lives by pain, we might possibly have been deprived of the poetry of Milton, the sculpture of Michelangelo, the oratorios of Handel, the paintings of Rembrandt, the music of Chopin. . . .

ह०

DIVINITY EXPRESSES itself not only through priests but also through great painters. Blessed with a Mount Everest of creative fire, their brushes fairly burst into flame. With poetry in their fingers and sunrises in their eyes, they cause Creation to begin anew. They touch their canvases into life that lasts a thousand years. Their studios are their temples. Every movement of their brushes is a hymn, and every color is the syllable of a psalm.

BELIEVING IN God is not a passport to a life devoid of suffering. It does not mean we are relieved of the fires of woe that burn in human hearts. It means enduring our trials hopefully, buttressed by the confidence that His companionship will never forsake us no matter what may betide. Believing in God means plunging into the storm, but pointing our compass toward the Light that cannot be dimmed by life's vicissitudes.

❧

RELIGION IS a hard taskmaster. It charges its devotees with duties and responsibilities that must never be shirked. But for him who is capable of carrying this burden, there waits a crown on earth that beggars the richest diadem worn by kings and queens and princes. Religion begins with a belief in God, but its compelling imperative is vindicated by a blueprint of behavior that looks to the redemption of all men everywhere. Only he is a co-worker with God who labors for the weal of God's children—the whole of mankind.

❧

WHAT ANTHEMS can compare with the tunes chirping out of a poplar tree that becomes the perch for sleepy birds at twilight, and then bares its breast for the moon to nestle in after the birds have dozed off to sleep?

OUR SONGS are not in vain. They will ultimately become a key to open the closed door of some heart that needs a song.

ॐ

SOMEWHERE BETWEEN the whippoorwill's sharp salutation to dawn and its vesper hymn to twilight, the consciousness of our Self merges with the consciousness of day. The atomic forces of the sunrays and the atomic forces within ourselves stem from one and the same Source. They create a unity that is terminated only when moonrays trip down the stairway of night for a few hours of courtship with the sleepy earth.

ॐ

IN THE geography of the spirit, all roads point in one direction—upward.

ॐ

WHAT MIRACLES can be wrought with hands! A baton encircled in Toscanini's fingers rules the wills of a hundred musicians in a symphony orchestra. His hands gesticulate gracefully like semaphores flashing messages from his enraptured soul to the souls of the players massed before him. They become more than hands—a textbook of poetry and rhythm, of force and tenderness, of passion and mystery . . .

MAN, CHILD of heaven, expends his strength in a fierce struggle to acquire earthly riches. When the contest is over and the tiara of success sits on his brow, he surveys his prizes and finds he has won—only earth.

৵

ESPOUSAL OF noble ideals, pursuit of truth, and performance of worthy acts, become the window through which an unobstructed view of the spirit may be gained.

৵

BEAUTY IS the mirror of God's countenance; music is the divine echo of His voice.

৵

THE NECROMANCY of beauty viewed with the eyes endures only for a few moments. Beauty that addresses itself to the soul beats a pathway to the God-image in man, which is eternal.

৵

WHEN LIFE is sheltered and safe, it becomes lonely. The mind that never dares is a blank cartridge that never hits a target.

WHEN FRAIL snowdrops, blooming in February, brave the white straitjackets of winter and hurl a defiant "I shall" at every chilling gust that commands "Thou shalt not," they testify to the futility of attempting to shackle the law of growth. Man's spirit must learn to cry "I shall" to tempests that too often evoke the cry of surrender, "I cannot."

❦

A CHILD who had learned how to tell time turned back the hands of the clock, believing he could thereby prolong the hour before it would be time to go to sleep.

❦

A MAN's philosophy will come tumbling down like a house of cards unless he learns that the bitterness of a No in life is needed no less than the sweetness of its Yes.

❦

WHILE THE desolate earth is tucked in with a blanket of snow, there is a beating within its heart, like a robin's wing, of the dormant miracle of Spring. The eye beholds a vast white kingdom, but under the surface countless orange, sapphire and vermilion braids are being woven for April's coronation gown.

WHEN THE spirit goes plodding through the icy blasts of a bleak December, it wistfully queries, "Where are the blooms of May and June?" Memory smiles, and in a trice barren gardens leap into flower and become visible to the mind's eye.

৯৶

PAINTING IS memory in color. Sculpture is memory in marble. Music is memory in song. Literature is memory in words. These murmur their afterglow in a dimension that laughs at time.

৯৶

As I listened to the haunting strains of Tchaikovsky, a wisp of violet cloud floated into the room and carried me on its back to the lonely snowflecked steppes of frozen Siberia.

৯৶

GREATER PRIZES are won by those who can forget than by those who must always remember.

৯৶

THE HIGHER we fuel the fire on the grates of knowledge the more clearly we see the innumerable secrets the mind has not even begun to fathom.

THE BLIND pianist stared out into black silence as he commenced his recital. But when his hands touched the keyboard they woke the keys into a seeing that illumined the hall with the shimmering of a thousand flames. With the eyes of his soul he saw far more than did his audience with their seeing eyes.

ॐ

DOES AUTUMN garb herself with exquisite garments as a masquerade to conceal her age and seek to reclaim the youth that was hers when she was Spring?

ॐ

EVERY QUESTION requires an answer, and every answer needs a question. Since life itself is a flaming questionmark, we ask far more than we answer. When life is only the answer, and no longer the question, it is time to close the book and let it gather dust on a shelf.

ॐ

ONCE I caught an errant wind chasing ivory shadows down the side of a tall spruce tree where sparrows were storing their little copper discs of song. When the spruce violently shook its shoulders, the wind fled but the discs of song remained.

THERE IS always room for a rainbow—either in a rain-drenched sky after a storm or in a tear-flooded heart after a deep hurt.

੪∾

A DREAM is an Aladdin's lamp waiting to light a pathway for things yet to be. It is the birthcry few can hear above the wailing and sobbing of a world in travail.

੪∾

BOTH STING and honey belong to a bee. The heart of man that is capable of love and benevolence also tents his cruelty and inhumanities.

੪∾

WHEN VIOLET buds begin to sprout, do their blue eyes reflect the hue of the sky, or does the cobalt sky mirror the blue of the violets?

੪∾

THOSE WHO whimper God is silent to their call are so deafened by the clamor of their own whining, they fail to hear the footfall of Deity walking by their side. There is no such thing as God's silence. Whatever silence exists is in man himself.

THE WHOLE world fails when a single heart's love fails.

෫ම

WHEN A man carries his ideals as an oak tree carries its acorns, he will some day see little stalks growing in soil which had been barren.

෫ම

MAN IS the product of God's workshop, and his soul is the authentic signature of the divine workmanship.

෫ම

THE HUMAN mind is an ivy plant that boldly climbs over every wall barring its way.

෫ම

LONG AND perilous is the journey from seed to flower. But what beauty and radiance the flowers store in their petaled knapsacks after they have passed from darkness to light!

෫ම

WILDFLOWERS ARE Nature's gypsies. They pitch their tents wherever there is a clod of earth willing to receive them.

EARTH RECONCILING herself that she must lie forever prostrate on her back, sends up flowers and trees to gain a closer view of heaven.

ᶻ❧

A MAN CAN quickly tell you how he employs his time. But what will his answer be when you ask him how he employs his soul?

ᶻ❧

LORD, LET my heart ever be a pathway over which my brother's pain may travel and not feel alone.

ᶻ❧

WHILE THE clock ticks the seconds away, they believe they are the whole of time.

ᶻ❧

BIRDCRIES ARE the echoed heartcries of earthbound men whose desires leap skyward out of their song-starved bodies.

ᶻ❧

LOVE THAT forgets how to give and knows only how to receive, is a caged eagle that no longer remembers the ecstasy of soaring through heights.

A LITTLE LAD who had become expert with a sling, took careful aim and brought down a bird with a single stone through the heart. He did not realize it was a song he had struck down and silenced forever.

&

FIREFLIES ARE the last lingering fragments of a fallen star that has lost its heaven but cannot bear to become a denizen of earth.

&

WHENEVER I SEE earth weighted down with a blanket of white snow, I remember what is on its underside, and I am willing to wait.

&

CLOUDS DO not vanish. They merely exchange their form from a mass of visible vapor floating above the earth into spectrum-tinctured blooms covering the earth.

&

SAID THE cloud to the sun, "I hold the ocean in my knapsack." Said the sun to the cloud, "I carry the day on my shoulders." Said the violet to cloud and sun, "I gather both of you into the ventricles of my heart and still find space for the stars."

THE HEAVIEST burden man carries through life is his Self strapped to his back.

ॐ

THE SCARS we bear testify to wounds that have healed. A wound unhealed does not yet form a scar.

ॐ

WHILE MEN lie intoxicated with the elixir of slumber, a Cosmic Gardener roams through the celestial meadow and plucks astral blooms. He wafts a single opalescent petal to earth, and in a twinkling it is dawn.

ॐ

OUR LIFE on this planet is a shadow of the unseen All-Life. Whatever is visible not only throws its own shadow, but is itself the shadow of something extrinsic to it.

ॐ

SKYLARKS DARTING heavenward on arrowed wings, hurl their rhapsodies earthward like musical hand grenades. Possessing neither voice nor wings, the flowers in their trenches laugh at the explosion and reply with transfiguring melodies of fragrance.

THE TREE casts a shadow on earth only when the sun's rays are caught in its boughs. There is no darkness that does not have a ray of light hovering somewhere nearby.

෨෧

EVERY TREE is a quotation mark citing God's call to man, "Stand up and reach toward Me!"

෨෧

TWO DECADES of Septembers ago I learned the deepest meaning of the law of growth. Standing on the summit of the Jungfrau in the Swiss Alps, I saw the Infinite carve its signature with indelible ink of timelessness on the mist-canyoned horizon where earth and sky became one. At that moment my soul leaped up in exaltation, stood on tiptoe, and I became more than I.

෨෧

OUR YEARS are migrating orioles nesting in our warm bodies for shelter overnight. In the morning they spread wings and mount the skyways that lead to Eternity.

෨෧

WHEN OUR thoughts curl up at our feet and purr like a drowsy kitten, they are soon forgotten. But when they snap at us like angry spaniels, their sharp teeth goad us to action.

HAD IT not stormed throughout the night, perhaps I might not have exclaimed cheerfully to my neighbor the next morning, "Isn't this a beautiful, balmy day?"

કસ

A VANDAL north wind ripped a swarm of threadbare leaves from their parent bough. They comforted each other with the deluding words, "See how we have forced the wind to take to his heels and run away."

કસ

A CANDLE CAN furnish light only by paying the price of slowly surrendering its life. Why should we fear to grow old if, while shedding our years, we shine through the darkness of some lonely life?

કસ

THE EVERLASTING God, mantled in Infinitude, can well afford the virtue of patience and forbearance. But when man, laden with a heartful of years and a few fragile hopes, learns how to wait, he clothes himself with a deific robe.

કસ

LIFE IS a bar of wayward music set to irregular beat. We are the thralled musicians singing its notes into a chorus of laughter, hope and pain.

WHEN THE scarlet fuel of roses spills out, there are scars of scorched oblivion where the petals had burned their fires. But when the wild delirium of April's anthem lulls the barren boughs to sing again, they kindle new budfires that will blaze into a greater red flame to guide the approaching feet of June.

ૐ

MAN LISTENS to a songbird's melody; heaven listens to the music of its flapping wings.

ૐ

WHENEVER I listen to the familiar dialogue of a tree communing with a visiting breeze, I wonder if their speech is the haunting echo of my forest ancestry.

ૐ

IN OUR PILGRIMAGE through life we converse with many, but we establish communication with only a precious few.

ૐ

IF IT WERE possible to unravel the soul like a ball of yarn, its final strip would never be reached. What would seem to be the end of the skein would in reality be the beginning, or source, where God's likeness was first woven into life's matrix.

FROM THE moment the storm struck with such suddenness late that August afternoon, I despaired that my phlox and larkspur, my delphinium and delicately belled fuchsia would survive its savage fury. But the next morning there they stood, showing not a single scar, while a hardy oak for whose safety I had not feared at all, lay sprawling like a paralyzed Goliath across my lawn. Who can understand the meaning of strength and weakness save one who has bared his heart to the ferocity of a storm!

ह

PSYCHOLOGY DEFINES man's fierce hunger to live as an expression of his instinct for self-preservation, and the definition is quite apt. But there are also those who, in a frenzy to gorge themselves on life, sink their greedy teeth so deeply into its flesh that they are unable to let go.

ह

DARKNESS LAMENTED to the sky: "What an intolerable burden I carry to be forever the handmaiden of night!" An eavesdropping star overheard the plaint, then looked down upon two lovers in each other's arms below and chuckled.

ह

IN SEEKING TO gain the verdict in your struggle with the world, ask how you fared in your struggle with yourself.

WHEN I return to stroll through the woodland I knew as a boy, I walk as though on holy ground, half-hoping to meet the selfsame winds that whispered sweet secrets to me in those enchanting days of early childhood.

ã❧

WHOEVER TRAMPLES on a living flower orphans the whole earth and pushes it back a step toward the void from which it emerged.

ã❧

A TREE WHOSE boughs are oversheltered from the inroads of winds, will bear leaves that will not have learned the language of song.

ã❧

MORNING-GLORIES AWAKEN as day's earliest blossoms, and the evening star is night's first golden bud. Out of what cosmic chrysalis did they receive this bidding to be the first to rush into bloom, the former heralding the terminus of night and the latter proclaiming the death-rattle of day?

ã❧

IS IT THE spark of dawn that wakes the bird to singing, or is it the tiny lightning-streak of music in the songbird's throat that kindles the night into dawn?

HISTORY ATTESTS that every time tyranny attempted to crush the blossom of Truth, its pollen scattered and fructified in regions the uncrushed flower might never have reached.

ह

LIFE LASHED Handel with scorpions of pain and with vipers of disease that blinded his eyes. He answered back with his immortal "The Messiah."

ह

A FIREFLY LIT on a blade of grass and whispered, "I will bring light to your darkness." The grass blade gazed toward the Milky Way overhead and remained silent.

PART TWO

Soulbeams

SONNETS

QUEST

So many cliffs we crossed,
Searched low and high,
To find the song we lost—
My heart and I.

On snow-clad peaks, in muted sound
Of dew, in pain,
My frantic quest I found
In vain, in vain . . . .

And now that years are long,
So wide apart,
I find the missing song
Locked in my heart.

SONG OF PAIN

What music haunts the earth's tormented brain,
What songs its throated fields and canyons sing
Through fluted choirs of breezes whispering
Transfiguring hymns that ripen seeds to grain!
What cosmic passion stirs the wild refrain
Of bouldered chorales whose cantatas wring
From barren winter madrigals of spring!
One alien air it spurns—the song of pain.

The song of pain is known alone to man—
Grief chants a mortal oratorio;
The heart composes in its fugitive span
Immortal music that outlives our woe.
No carol earth has sung since time began
Can rival canticles our sorrows grow.

TIDES OF TIME

Unnumbered hosts of vanished centuries
Have trod this sunken path since Time began,
Have leapt across duration's shoreless span
Into the bottom of oblivion's seas.
No clattering, no heraldry of breeze
Or storm proclaimed this tramping caravan
That watched the anthropoid grow into man
Spurning the earth to seek eternities.

Unnumbered tides of Time will ebb and flow,
Become Today then noiseless disappear,
But every New Year's eve sees humans grow
Tumultuous with horns that blast the ear—
As if one needs this blatant din to know
That life is orphaned of another year.

FLAME-CLAD

Our final couch is in the valley. There
We slumber undisturbed by sharp desire,
The kith and kin of shriveled rose and briar.
So ends the clay. But flame-clad spirits dare
To build in heights: the gabled roof, the stair,
The arch and steeple, pinnacle and spire,
Are outward patterns of the inner fire
That leaps beyond our structures—in the air.

What triumph if we conquer steel and stone?
When granite pillars cover beam and spar,
And towers hurl their shoulders to the sky,
We fashion domes of vision from our own
Soul-quarry, and outsoar the farthest star
To loftier citadels our dreams espy.

TRANSITION

Upon this terrace two full moons ago
A snarling monster, Frost, held life at bay,
Clawed fiercely at my garden starved for prey
And lapped the soil with savage tongues of snow.
Now I must doubt credulity, for lo!
Two honeyed lilac bushes bar the way,
Besiege the air with fragrance as they sway
Their purple-blossomed clusters to and fro.

How lavishly the hands of Nature fling
Rich toys to every season, parent-wise:
Verbena-quilted cribs to infant Spring;
Rose-petaled shawls to Summer, lapis skies;
To Autumn vivid paints for coloring
A masterpiece of beauty as she dies!

BEETHOVEN

His soul was tuned to music few can hear:
Symphonic fragrance strumming from a rose,
Primeval pines in forest studios
Composing rhapsodies for vale and weir.
He was a lyre divine whose muted ear
Heard arias in silent dew and snows,
Found chansons in each dawn that overflows
The ebon shores of night's unbounded sphere.

When suns are burned to ash through ageless shining,
And comets blanch from pouring out their fire,
When twilight spires are stripped of copper lining
And cadence fails the touch of hand to lyre,
Beethoven's harp will sate the cosmic pining
For lyric paeans to make the heart aspire.

SILENCES

We cannot feel the breath of flowers, yet
We know they breathe. We cannot hear the speech
Of pregnant blossoms, but we know they teach
Life's holiest law through fruit-tongued floweret,
More eloquent than words we soon forget.
Too deep for sentient feeling, they upreach
Their petaled hands in silent prayer and preach
From texts inscribed in Nature's alphabet.

Her deepest truths are culled in silences:
The fall of dew; the hush of moonrise; snow;
Day tripping down the stairs of dawn; the hands
Of Spring outflanking Winter's fortresses;
A rose in bloom. These Nature's secrets know,
All these, and silent love that understands.

PAIN HAS ITS PURPOSE, TOO

Pain has its purpose, too. The anguished breast
Responds with dirges to batons of woe,
Like naked desert sands where wild winds blow
Shrill elegies that cannot be suppressed.
Blind Milton knew. A quenchless light possessed
His shrouded orbs, unlatched the portico
Of endless night and taught his soul to know:
"Who best bear his mild yoke, they serve him best."

Life's delicate harp vibrates with many strings,
And blends a melody of mingled strains
Into a paean of rhythmic harmony.
Not merely bliss upsoars on music's wings,
Not joy alone intones the soul's refrains—
Pain, too, must chorus in life's symphony.

HUMAN NATURE

Ten million eons after time began,
When galaxies of white-hot suns were hurled
From deep immensities that draped the world,
A brutish creature grew from ape to man.
Down through the gulf of time's unmeasured span
He scanned the roofless vault where planets whirled,
Until his darkly caverned mind unfurled
The civilizing banner of the clan.

Now ocean deep in science and in lore,
He matches God with his inventive skill;
But once the bugles summon him to war
The snarling jungle instinct rules him still,
And he becomes the savage beast once more,
Much less a man than ape bent on the kill.

GOSPEL

How futile man's attempt to sate his need
For God in creeds and bibles! Let him scan
The living script that Nature writes, and read
How God Himself records His need for man.
In braided filigree of bloom and leaf,
In dawns and starshine, cadenced lake and wood,
In glaciered mountains and in coral reef
He strains to make His hunger understood.

For whom this vast unfoldment of His might,
This drama of creation without end?
For whom this cosmic theme of growth and light,
If not for man whom He yearns to befriend?
Let man who needs a scripture for his eyes
Peruse the star-built altars in the skies!

ANTIQUE SHOP

This is his raptured world, where he can stand
Among his paintings, rugs and tapestries,
Surrounded by antiques from many a land,
And feel the heartbeat of the past. He sees
A poem in quaintly patterned furniture,
And every crevice in a wornout chair
Becomes a siren mouth with song to lure
Him back to vanished ages time laid bare.

What stirring panoramas greet him here!
What eerie incense to his nostrils strays
As shrouded years, long silent, reappear
And reminisce of buried yesterdays,
While olden clocks whose builders long are gone
Chime echoes of their hearts that pulsate on!

SCULPTURE

See how the drudging cobbler's back is bent
Over his last, how for a crust of bread
And bowl of pottage day by day is spent
In pounding, pounding shoes for men to tread.
Then see the sculptor's eager eyes aflame,
As pounding, pounding mallet fashions clay
To plastic molds of sculpture that reclaim
In marble what the tomb will store away.

Capricious fate, by what imperative
Have you ordained this law we cannot shirk:
That some must toil because they crave to live,
And some must live because they yearn to work!
Be patient, cobbler, wait! Some day your dust
Will sculpture seeds into a floral bust.

LAMENT OF THE TREES

Ah God! Is there no respite from our woe?
Why, like Prometheus, must we be bound
By manacles of roots that twine below
And tether us with twisted ropes of ground?
You gave us knotted arms to embrace the sun,
To fraternize with errant winds, to peep
Into the wine-tinged vault when day is done,
But from our dungeon, earth, we cannot creep.

How vain your murmuring, a Voice replies,
Man's fragile life will answer your lament.
Half-soil, half-soul, he seeks the highest skies
And dares to touch the Throne though earthen bent.
The lives of men and trees intone the paean:
Upward, upward toward the empyrean!

HOW SHALL I SING

How shall I sing of dawns and canopies
That croon cadenzas set to cosmic notes,
How shall I put in verse the minstrelsies
That undulate in linnets' raptured throats!
How vain to fashion odes, compose refrains
Of whirling spheres and serenading stars,
When furrowed earth intones such lulling strains
That golden grain comes waltzing from her scars!

I sing of things finite, of man. My songs
Hold tears of children, plaints of prostrate souls,
The brittle hopes and joys of toiling throngs
Whom gold allays, a crust of bread cajoles.
Their psalms of laughter, pain and grief combine
In human rhapsodies of the Divine.

IMMORTALITY

This racing blood, these lungs, this heart
Transmuting oxygen to living breath,
Will turn to stone, unsentient and apart,
Grafted upon the marble skin of death.
No vestige will survive of flesh or brain,
No residue of marrow or of mind,
Only an afterglow of love and pain
Brooding in hearts of those I leave behind.

Yet, when this kneeling earth beneath my feet
Becomes my bed, is there not more than this,
More than a tortuous journey sadly fleet
That winds its way to some unknown abyss?
The Now and Here, this bodied part of me,
Are shells that hold the pearl, Infinity.

CARDINAL

All day the pelting storm, and through the night
A howling wind-horde at my window pane,
As if intent to match their snarling might
With the purling accents of the falling rain.
All day again the dull monotonous dripping
Of raindrops nesting in the flooded eaves,
Until near dusk I saw the sunlight slipping
Its copper sabre through the listless leaves.

A dauntless cardinal with wings of fire
Darted in arrowed flight into a tree,
A scarlet symbol of the flamed desire
To transmute teardrops into melody.
And now when rain of woe falls overlong,
The thought of crimson wings hymns into song.

TWILIGHT CIRCUS

Across the grottoes of the western sky
A circus caravan meanders by.
Calliopes with wheels of topaz rays
Are drawn by copper stallions, manes ablaze,
While monster dragons, fowl and snarling beast,
In shapes fantastical, lazuli fleeced,
Parade into the twilight's waning light
Until they reach the sawdust tents of night.

An audience of stars convulsed with mirth
Looks down amused upon our comic earth,
Making me wonder what had brought them glee—
The clouds with their grotesque buffoonery,
Or we who strut like puppets here below
And form a circus that we do not know?

PART THREE

Nocturnes

LYRICS

Not for the swift and strong
Upsoars my tremulous song;
Those who can laugh with time
Have little need for rhyme.

But faltering souls that cling
Like birds with broken wing
To walls they cannot scale
With ladders of travail

To hearts that wait in vain,
Whose only poems are pain,
To those whom song passed by
These hope-winged lyrics cry.

NOCTURNE

Dusk enhalos the sun's red mane
And daubs the hills with violet foam,
In nests of my heart white doves of longing
Are winging for home.
Beneath my feet the earth's heart pulses,
Veined with blood from poppy and rose,
While quills of gloaming pencil a stillness
The spirit knows.

A nightjar perched on a hemlock bough,
Throttled by silence the whole day long,
Fills the flagons of night with the wine
Of his churring song.
Roaming above the reticent grasses,
Glowworms heave their lances of gold;
Invisible sylphs in chariots of breezes
Ride through the wold.

The jacinth clouds are laid away
In ebon caskets beneath the sky;
The lonely song of the mateless nightjar
Is a hermit cry.
But in my heart the doves of longing
Spread frail wings in restless flight,
And flood the vats of my deepest being
With the music of night.

COVENANT

Oft in the black-foamed night's Alone,
When trampling herds of winds bemoan
Their homelessness with a plaintive lowing,
And tribes of shadows mill around
Wrangling for every acre of ground,
I can feel the dark world growing.

When the starry choir trills a lullaby
To the purple silence that cradles the sky,
I can hear the looms of darkness weaving
Translucent skeins for tomorrow's sun,
And deep in my heart I sense the cleaving
Of earth's great heart bursting with dawn.

Linked with the beat of my pulsing blood,
In concert with Nature's brotherhood,
Throbs the vibrant breath of things to be;
I scatter dream-white seeds of light
In the fertile soil of my Brother night,
And wait for our sun-sired progeny.

Oft in the brooding night's Alone,
Flesh of my flesh, bone of my bone,
I can feel the dark world grow;
The night and I psalm a rhythmic chant
That joins us in a covenant
More binding than any pact I know.

LET THE SOLITARY HEART

Let the solitary heart,
Wandering knee-deep in hunger,
Climb the jutting rocks
Of its granite hills;
Let it bare its breast
To the speeding red arrow
Released by the archer's bow
In the west.

Let it mount the stairway
Of the blurred sunset,
And watch the stealthy darkness
Come prowling from the south;
Then gaze at the gargoyle of time
Grinning in purple silence,
As spawning tides of night
Drool out of its mouth.

Let its throbbing wait
For bronzed doors to open
Across the shadowy lagoon
In the sea of the dark,
Until ivory atoms of sunlight
Drive away the nothingness
That rose high above
Its low-water mark.

Shall the wandering heart
Find its own sea level
By flowing inward or outward
In the twilight flood?
Shall it upraise its head
Or lower its eyes,
As time goes drifting
In the seaweed of its blood?

HIDDEN ROOTS

There are roots the soul grows,
Deeper than earth can sprout,
Lifebuds with vintage richer
Than the tinctured scarlet
Scraped from a rose
When its time runs out.

Behold the cloistered seedlings
Breaking loose from the ground,
With wreaths of petaled color
To garland every mound.
Then look to the cratered heart
Gardened with crowded seeds,
Some erupting bloom-fire
From lava of desire,
Others stillborn, set apart
In the womb of its needs.

Daily the throng mills around,
Moving ponderous or fleet,
Trampling the fecund ground
With indifferent feet;
Unheeding the miracle
Of hidden roots sipping
Earth's eternal sweet wine,
Or the soul's decanters

Ceaselessly dripping
Potions of the Divine.

Grow upward, soul and seed,
Into man, into grain, into tree,
But ponder your affinity
With the roots on which you feed.
Dance to the impassioned song
Of hunger, sun and dew
That caroled since your birth,
But never forget the lullaby
Of roots that cradled you
In the womb, in the earth!

DANCE OF THE LEAVES

How mournful brood these faded leaves
Beneath the boughs that gave them breath,
How frayed the threadbare coat they wear,
Ripped by the vandal claws of death!

With rapier thrusts the North Wind stabs,
Howling with ice-fanged petulance
To snatch the leaves in eddying gusts
And whirl them in a ghostly dance.

Around and round they pirouette,
Convulsed in a fantastic waltz,
Alone, in twos, in threes and fours
They plunge in headlong somersaults.

Then suddenly the wind abates
And silences its weird refrain;
It lays aside its mad baton—
The dancers are dead leaves again.

DISTANCE

No human ear can hearken
The call of star to star;
Ah, who can list to language
From firmaments so far?

I stand beside her gravestone,
Seek words to heal my scar;
But though she is so near me,
She is so far, so far . . . .

O spacious stars above me,
Too far to utter sound,
More distant is her chamber
Two metres underground!

EAVES

Gay are the pyramid spikes of the lilacs,
Clusters of purple erupting in fire,
Stars haunt the earth disguised as jonquils,
Thrushes are tuning their lyre.
Somnolent woodlands are stretching their limbs,
Orchards bestir from their slumber,
Bloom-starved gardens without number
Breakfast on morsels of sun.

There! see the redbird, clad in sunrise,
Darting from roof to roof!

Restlessly, wearily, frustrate,
He searches in vain, in vain
For the familiar eaves
Where he has lain
With his mate.

Frenzied he calls, but every call
Is answered by a deafening hush
More silent than a snowflake's fall,
More silent than a poppy's flush,
More silent than the lilac grows;
And then he knows, he knows
That last Spring's eaves
Lie buried under last Fall's leaves,

And he, convulsed, disconsolate,
On the octaved scale of his ache,
Pours out his heart in singing lest it break.

Through all our years we sky
The redbird's flight within ourselves.

Like him we dart on tremulous wings of longing
Toward alcoves where the heart had built a nest,
But find them littered with alien eggs
That hatch to mocking magpies in our breast.
What is a life whose hunger is eaves,
This span that is heart-beat thin,
We perch upon the outer doorway,
We seldom enter in.

SING TO ME SONGBIRD

Sing to me, songbird, wake up the fields,
Unburden your heart in showers of song,
The carols you warble pound in my brain
The whole night long.

Empty the music that stifles your throat,
The memory of sky that clings to your wings,
For yours is a chant from beginning to end
My own life sings.

The moment you scatter your arrows of song
I know they are mine, a theme I have heard,
What cries out of you would cry out of me
If I were a bird.

For you are myself and I am yourself,
We perch together on music's plateau;
Our hearts must perish unless we can sing,
I know, I know.

PRIMAL

Go deeper than sound,
Search farther than sight,
Blast beneath the quarry
Of the heart's naked rock;
Stoke the embered mind
Brighter than sun or star,
Until you discover
The primal thing you are.

There are layers of Self
Dimensioned like grass,
Thin as your image
In a looking-glass;
Yet behind the image
Is the foetal core
Of your greater Self
You never knew before.

Mine the hidden ore
Beneath the stone,
Probe beyond the ridges
Of brain and bone;
Then sift the debris
Of hearing and seeing,
And behold the universe
That cradles your being.

PREMONSTRATION

This room is an eerie world—
Four green walls and a paneled door,
Zinc-white ceiling and parquet floor;
And cluttered in between,
Bookshelves and a record player
Behind a Chinese screen,
With harlequins in masquerade
And dragons etched in jade.

On this sequestered isle of books
I throb the charcoal nights away.
An electric clock gyrating round
Spirals time with a droning sound;
Scheherazade on my record player
Strips the silence bare—
The dragons stir, the harlequins sigh,
This room is a suburb of Shanghai.

Then vaguely I half remember
The contour of a forgotten dream,
When my life was not yet life
And this self was not yet me.
I recall moonfire on a stream,
Myself beneath a mulberry tree,
With myriad rose-lidded eyes
Abloom in oriental skies.

I wonder if somewhere in time
Someone will squat in a hoveled room
With muddied walls, a hole for a door,
Thatched ceiling and an earthen floor
In a hemisphere oceans away;
And half remembering the things I see,
Will peer across eons of ricefields
And discover a kinship with me.

MIGRANT THRUSH

He must have adored this elderbush!
For a cluster of years the migrant thrush
Flew to these branches out of the south
With orisons psalming from his mouth.
One day the berries would smile into bud
And all of a sudden—there he stood!

Who can tell what wisdom or sight
Guided his straight-as-arrow flight,
What magical currents of atmosphere
Directed his wings to haven here?
But I know each April he poured out to me
His pent-up cascades of melody,
Sundered the curtains of morning apart
With silver flutings out of his heart.

April is here and the bush is bare,
Not of foliage but his singing there;
And now it seems an act profane
For the callous berries to ripen again,
To string their beads of ruby-red
On familiar boughs where he made his bed.

Each soughing breeze is a vesper bell
That clears its throat and tolls farewell,
Whispers laments for the splintered wing

That answers no more the music of Spring.
An ache and loneliness deluge my soul
For the muted voice, the broken bowl;
How can I suffer to see it go
When song is the life of the life I know!

JANUARY DAY

The burnt-out stump of a January day
Smoulders across the torpid landscape,
Like a lighted cigarette tossed away,
Still smoking, curling blue haze about,
But instant by instant burning out.
Four o'clock, reads the watch on my wrist
Where seconds go racing under a glass,
But the ticking in my blood, in my mind,
Geared to a clock I shall never rewind,
Tolls the hour of midwinter.

Winter days are old hearts reminiscing,
Tired parcels of earth that sit and reflect;
Their inner stethoscopes detect
The throbbing pulse behind the bleakness,
The palpitant heartbeat under the nude.
In this frozen soil that gamboled with rain,
Violets will rise from their graves again,
And seeds, embalmed in ice, mildewed,
Will hoard in the skull of the earth
A new dream of rebirth.

June stood here and unpacked her roses,
Filled her cisterns with petaled foam,
Then kneeling on acres trampled threadbare
Seized sulking roots and seeds by the hair

And dragged them out of their catacomb.
Then came October, set fire to the trees
And burned their leaves to a copper mold,
Thrust daggers of frost into stem and vein
And plundered their will to live again,
Leaving them prostrate, cold.

Now January hobbles on feet of snow
Over whitened graves with stealthy tread
Of the lately living and the lately dead;
Yearning for flocks that feathered the sky,
For the katydids' chirp and the robins' cry,
For the chorals sung a summer ago.
The winds look up and howl with laughter
As slanting sunrays with shadows long
Show January's teeth furtively nibbling
The bones of summer's song.

MINUET OF DEW

Ears that have hearkened to cannons of thunder
Bombing the sky through and through,
Hunger for music that pulses from silence
Of canticles chorused by dew.

Silence that lulls from underground choirs
Lyrics of fruit newly born,
Chanting red flames into travailing blossoms,
And bronze into tassels of corn.

Softly, how softly the dew-fountains shower
Milk in the breasts of the earth;
See with what eager insistence they carol
Incredible secrets of birth!

Sing, magic dew, with your viols of silence
Arias of growth to the dust;
Drench every furrow with palpitant music
That urges: You must, you must!

FIRE

Once it is touched by fire,
Nothing remains the same;
Whether the furnaced heart
Singed by coals of desire,
Or lighted fagots of thought
Sparks of truth have caught,
Once it has known the flame,
Nothing is ever the same.

Formless, shapeless, it paws
Toward its primal origin,
Seeking with probing claws
The presence beneath the skin.
Meteors, forests and breath,
All that is young or hoar,
Melts when raped by its arson
To the something it was before.

The redbird's blazing wing,
The flaming rose and my soul,
Are fractioned sparks that sing
In the choir of its dazzling whole.
In vain is man's desire
To flee the fatal fire
And set himself apart—
Since the fire is his heart.

ICARIAN LEAF

Pity a fallen leaf
With the wind inside,
Raised from the dust
By a sudden gust
That sweeps it wide
From the parent tree;
With no memory
Of ever dying,
Harboring an illusion
Of a bird flying.

Beguiled leaf
Winging over space,
Forswear this dream of height,
Of tilting your face
In upward flight.
There is no tomorrow
For the pinions you borrow
To soar from the bough;
Only a wind can reach you now,
Nothing more.
Give up your dance macabre,
This frenzy to soar;
Living for you
Is a bolted door.

Icarian leaf
Clutching at lean air,
Are you unaware
It is only the wind
Not yourself that flies?
How can flight call
To a thing that dies?
Leaf in the air,
Heart in despair,
Fall, fall!

DROUTH

First the fruit trees then the grain,
Droop in a coma panting for rain;
Orchards lie stupored, desolate, wan,
Blistered with fever by the blazing sun.
Even the streams are all out of breath,
Their skeletoned beds as naked as death.

Summer has flamed like a forest fire,
Scorching the fields to a funeral pyre;
The half-living cattle roam in a mass
Nibbling at briars and invisible grass,
While moaning dogs go staggering
In search of a puddle or trickling spring.

Not a wren or meadow-lark opens its mouth
To break the hush of the murderous drouth;
Only the rain-crows fidget and croak
As famined earth and animals choke,
And starving herons stand mutely by,
Waiting, waiting their turn to die.